How To Make The Perfect Quiche

Denise Hawley

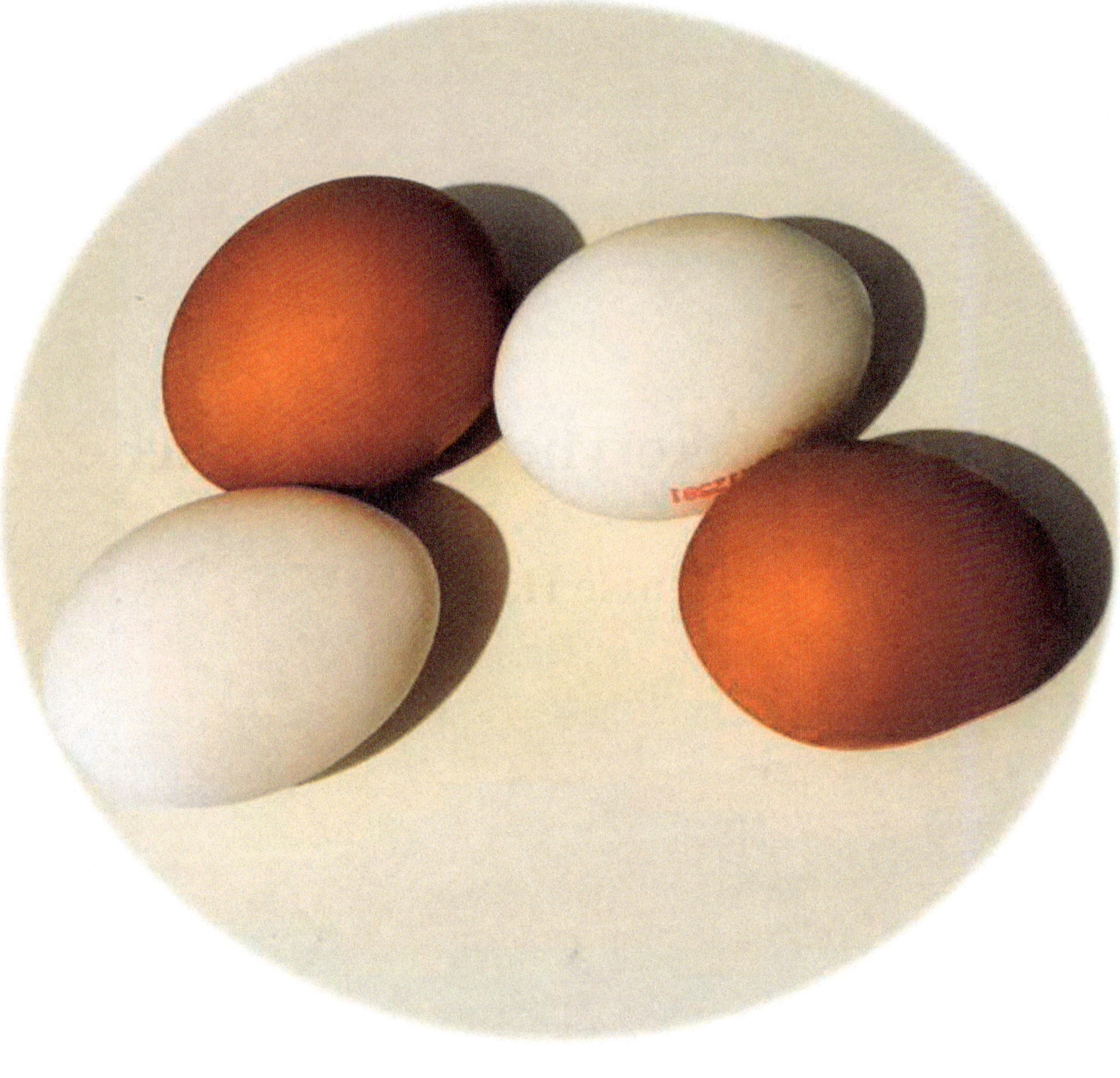

How To Make The Perfect Quiche
by
Denise Hawley

First edition 19th November 2023

Copyright Denise Hawley 2023
ISBN: 979-886255415-1

Denise Hawley has asserted the right to be identified as the author of this work under the Copyright, Designs and Patents Act 1988.

All Rights Reserved

No part of this publication may be reproduced, stored in or introduced into a retrieval system, or transmitted in any form or by any means, electronic, mechanical, photocopying, recording or otherwise without the prior written permission of the publisher and copyright owners.

Bonne Fille Publishing Company
London ~ Norwich ~ Los Angeles

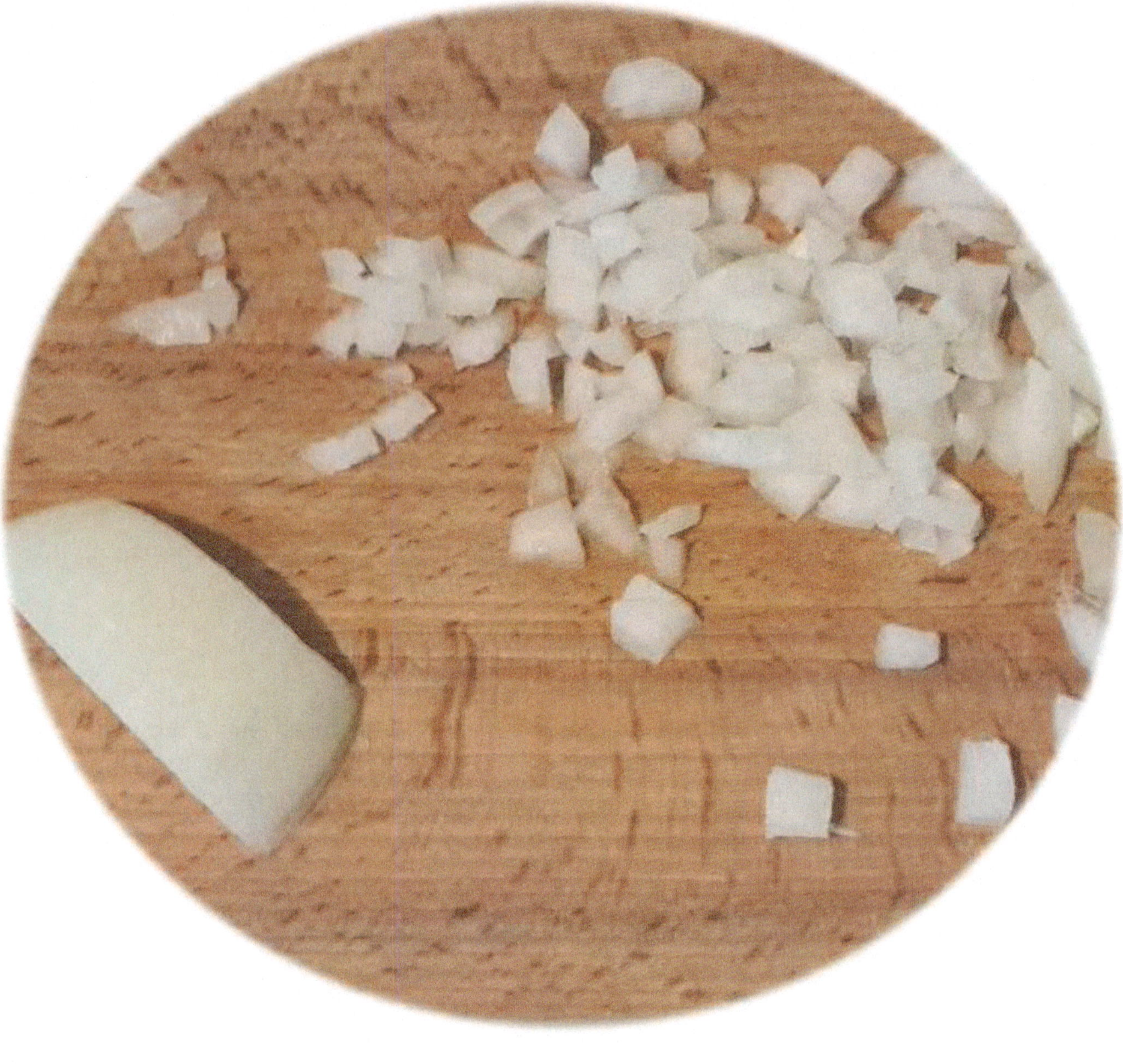

Contents

Start With The Right Equipment 7
Three Layers:
    The Crust (Method) 9
Recipes 22
    The Crust (Recipe) 23
    The Custard 24
    Quiche Lorraine 25
    Spinach and Ricotta Quiche 26
    German Bratwurst Quiche 28
    Chicken Kebab Quiche 30
    Salami and Gorgonzola Quiche 32
    Masala Quiche 34
    Quiche Rancheros 36
    Spicy Spanish Quiche 38
    Courgette (Zucchini) and Cheese Quiche 40
    Club Quiche 42
    Cheese and Tomato Quiche 44
    Chicken and Avocado Quiche 46
    Four Cheese Quiche 48
    Cheddar Mushroom Quiche 50
    Roasted Vegetable Quiche 52

Caprese Quiche	54
Greek Olive and Goat Cheese Quiche	56
Cajun Quiche	58
Savoury Pumpkin Quiche	60
Pumpkin Pie Spice	61
Pumpkin Pie	62
Custom Quiche	64
A World of Possibilities	67
Notes	68

Start With The Right Equipment

Every country has that one dish that evolved from using up leftovers. Quiche started out as one of these catch-all dishes, but over time has become a gourmet speciality so delectable that the French and Germans both claim to have invented it!

Now there are many books on the market who compete to tell you they will give you the highest number of recipes to make quiche. If you're like me, you will never make most of them, but may find a favourite or a few that you like to make from among them. I will give you only a few recipes, but I will teach you to adapt those into making a magnificent quiche from anything that you want to!

They say that it is a poor craftsman who blames his tools, but I would modify this to say that an expert craftsman collects the right tools! So with that in mind, let's begin with the basic equipment you will need;

Measuring cup   fork
measuring spoons   A medium-sized mixing bowl
wire whisk   spoons if needed
table knife   kitchen scale (if required)

And most important of all, an attractive quiche dish and a pastry cutter.

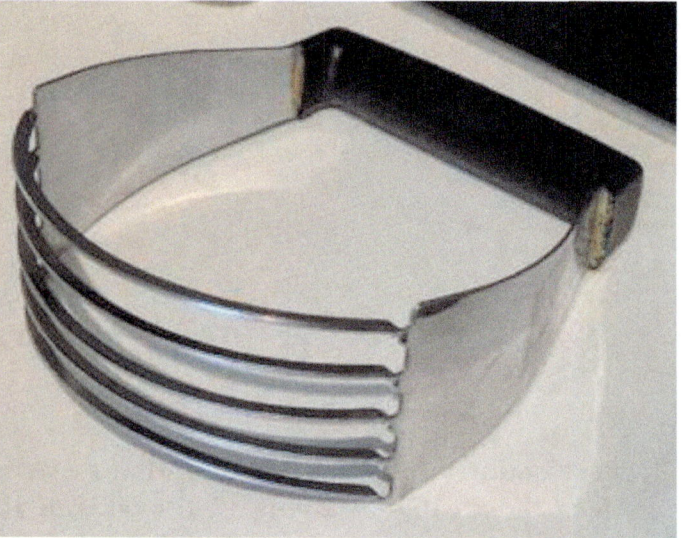

Personally, I prefer a ceramic dish. They have a classical quality to them that makes for a good presentation. Metal dishes that allow you to remove the pan and let the quiche stand on its own have their merits, but nothing says *French country kitchen* like a glazed ceramic finish.

When making pastry, texture is the key. To make a quiche crust with just the right flaky quality requires three things; the right types and amounts of fat, a good pastry cutter like the one pictured above, and getting your hands into the mix. We will come to that soon.

Many recipes tell you to substitute using two knives for cutting the fat into the flour mixture. When you look at the price of a proper pastry cutter in your local supermarket, you will wonder why you tormented yourself with so much extra work. They are as cheap as any mixing spoon and worth every penny, even if you use them only once in a while.

As in all baking, the final product will reflect your care and attention to the quality of ingredients and to the basic methods. With that in mind, let's talk about the crust.

Three Layers: The Crust

This crust is especially for quiche, nothing else. A recipe that tells you to use an ordinary pie crust or to buy a refrigerated pre-made crust is a recipe for mediocrity. For a perfect quiche, you need a perfect crust. Fortunately, it is exceptionally easy to make.

For one thing, there is no rolling and juggling to keep the crust together while laying it in the quiche dish. This crust is pressed into place. You literally cannot go wrong! Also if you get the fat to flour mixture right, it will be the most perfectly flaky quiche crust you have ever encountered.

The secret to quiche is to think of it in three layers; the crust, the filling and the custard. I will give you the recipes for the crust and custard first because these remain the same for most of the recipes included in this book. Slight variations in spices for the custard might be desired, but otherwise these layers remain the same. The fillings, on the other hand, can vary widely.

So, let's begin with your medium-sized mixing bowl. A quick word to the wise; most of the objects you use for the crust will be re-used at the custard stage, so don't throw them into the sink too quickly! For example, if you are making a basic Quiche Lorraine, your first step is to fry the bacon. Keep the fork you use for turning it as you can use it again for piercing the crust with holes, then again for some of the mixing at the custard stage.

Quiche Crust Recipe

1 cup + 2 Tbsps All Purpose [Plain] Flour
Pinch salt
3 Tbsps cold butter
3 Tbsps Vegetable Shortening [Stork Margarine]
2 -5 Tbsps Cold Milk
1 egg white

Stir a generous pinch of salt into flour in a medium bowl.

Using pastry cutter, cut in butter and shortening until it appears fine and grainy.

Rub the fat into the flour until it is thoroughly incorporated. It should resemble a fine dust.

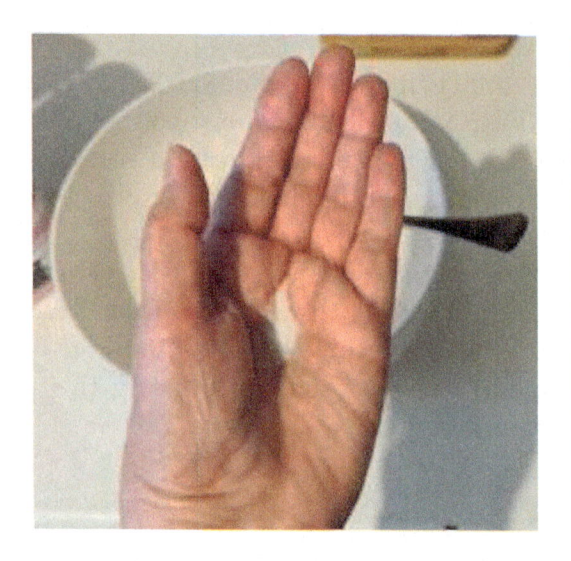

Sprinkle 2 Tablespoons cold milk evenly over flour and fat mixture.

Stir with a fork. If you used a fork to cook bacon, this one will work fine and add a slight taste of bacon to the pastry.

Add 1 spoon cold milk at a time and mix until pressing on the dough with the fork makes it stick together. The less milk you use, the lighter the pastry will turn out.

If you've used enough fat, it should be sticky enough by around 3 spoons to continue. Don't exceed 5!

Pour mixture into Quiche dish and press to bottom and sides. Don't leave it too thick. About 3/8 inch [3mm] is ideal. Be sure to keep the bowl aside to use again.

You don't have to press it all the way up the sides, but be sure to press into the groove so that it isn't too thick.

Pierce the pastry all over with the same fork you used to mix the dough.

Some might try to flake off. Work carefully, pressing pieces back if necessary. This is a good sign your pastry will be flaky as well.

Separate your smallest egg, dropping the white onto the pastry and the yolk into your mixing bowl. The other eggs will join it soon.

Gently spread the egg white over the pierced pastry, covering the entire surface.

You are now ready to add your filling.

Adding The Filling

The important thing to remember about the filling is most items need to be pre-cooked first. Any meat or vegetable items should be in ready to eat form, so items like onions or mushrooms may be exceptions.

Lets use a classic Quiche Lorraine as an example. Cooking the bacon is the first thing I do when I make one of these, followed by cutting the onions and grating the cheese. If I have any in supply, I find spring onions [green onions] provide the best flavour, but basic white, yellow or brown onions are nice too.

Sprinkle your filling ingredients evenly over the crust.

Next is the cheese.

Grating it makes it easy to spread across the other ingredients, though soft cheeses would be easier to dollop closely around the dish as you would for a pizza with goat cheese or Ricotta.

Grated cheese can also be used for topping the quiche. When baking is finished, spread grated cheddar across the top and bake for five more minutes or until cheese is melted. Be careful when serving! A layer of melted cheese holds the heat!

Once your filling ingredients are in place, it's time to add the custard. Whip up your eggs and the saved yolk with a fork and add any seasonings. For Quiche Lorraine, I use 1/4 teaspoon garlic granules (not salt!) and 1/8 teaspoon ground nutmeg. The nutmeg improves the flavour of any quiche custard, but leave it out if you don't like it.

An old chef's trick for adding spices if you're familiar enough with amounts to forego measuring spoons is to pour the spices into the lid of the jar, so you can tip some back if you accidentally spill out too much.

Mix in thoroughly before adding the milk. Continue to whip eggs while adding the milk to mix the seasonings well. Pour slowly while beating with the fork. It's best to pre-heat the oven for a few minutes while you're busy with this stage.

Start the oven at gas mark 7 [450 F, 220 C]

Many quiche recipes call for heavy cream, but I find that full fat [whole] milk actually works better to achieve a fluffy custard. Don't use low fat or skimmed milk as the fat content isn't sufficient to thicken into a good custard. You don't want it to come out watery!

Carefully place the quiche dish in pre-heated, hot oven. The milk will slosh easily, so use two hands and slide slowly onto rack in the middle of the oven. Take note of the time or set a timer. You absolutely must turn down the heat after 10 minutes!

Reduce heat to gas mark 4 [300 F, 150 C] and allow to bake 30-40 minutes, until golden brown on top and a knife inserted into the middle comes out clean. Remove from oven and allow to cool 10 minutes before serving.

You now have an amazing quiche!

I recommend serving with side salads or new potatoes, though you might have other ideas of your own!

Also, some creative quiches can be given to different accompaniments, like the Hacienda Quiche you'll find in the recipes to follow. Perhaps refried beans or tortilla chips would go well with this one.

Quiche is versatile and ethnic variations are open to your wildest imagination.

Recipes

Part of the beauty of quiche is that most of them use the same basic crust and custard, with a few exceptions like the Savoury Pumpkin Quiche (page 34).

The following nine recipes cover a range of international options that usually don't show up in other quiche recipe books or especially in general recipe books that might contain one or two quiche options.

The classic Quiche Lorraine is essential of course, and I've followed this with my own favourite Spinach and Ricotta Quiche. Already at this stage I want to emphasise the simplicity of substitutions to suit your own taste. Don't like Ricotta cheese? Spinach and cheddar works very well. Perhaps goat cheese for a more Mediterranean taste. Add some olives if you like!

The stronger flavours and international quintessence of Salami and Gorgonzola, Masala or Cajun Quiche offer unique options for a meal with a difference, and the Mexican spices in Quiche Rancheros can be adjusted to your own level of spiciness.

Pumpkin Quiche is included to demonstrate that unusual choices can work very well, but the real glory of this book is in the Custom Quiche, where YOU choose what you want to include in your special meal. After all, quiche was originally one of those dishes where leftovers found a new vitality.

Quiche Crust Recipe

1 cup + 2 Tbsps All Purpose [Plain] Flour
Pinch salt
3 Tbsps cold butter
3 Tbsps Vegetable Shortening [Stork Margarine]
2 -5 Tbsps Cold Milk
1 egg white

Stir a generous pinch of salt into flour in a medium bowl.
Using pastry cutter, cut in butter and shortening until it appears fine and grainy.
Rub the fat into the flour until it is thoroughly incorporated. It should resemble a fine dust.

Sprinkle 2 Tablespoons cold milk evenly over flour and fat mixture.
Stir with a fork. If you used a fork to cook bacon, this one will work fine and add a slight taste of bacon to the pastry.

Add 1 spoon cold milk at a time and mix until pressing on the dough with the fork makes it stick together. The less milk you use, the lighter the pastry will turn out.

If you've used enough fat, it should be sticky enough by around 3 spoons to continue. Don't exceed 5!

Pour mixture into Quiche dish and press to bottom and sides. Don't leave it too thick. About 3/8 inch [3mm] is ideal. Be sure to keep the bowl aside to use again.

You don't have to press it all the way up the sides, but be sure to press into the groove so that it isn't too thick.

Basic Quiche Custard

       3 medium eggs
       1 egg yolk
       1 cup milk (full fat, whole)
       Seasonings to taste*

Whip up your eggs and the saved yolk with a fork and add any seasonings.

Mix in thoroughly before adding the milk. Continue to whip eggs while adding the milk to mix the seasonings well. Pour slowly while beating with the fork. It's best to pre-heat the oven for a few minutes while you're busy with this stage.

* For most quiches, I recommend 1/4 teaspoon garlic granules and pinch of ground nutmeg. Some recipes will specify specific seasonings instead.

* Note that an American cup is 8 fluid ounces. This equates to about 227 millilitres. You can, however, estimate these amounts with a standard size coffee mug.

One cup of fluid will come to about 1-inch or 3 centimetres below the top of the mug.

Estimates are close enough for the milk in a quiche. After all, eggs vary in volume.

For flour, you'll want to be more careful as the flour to fat ratio will affect the texture of the crust.

Quiche Lorraine

Ingredients:

For crust:

1 cup + 2 Tbsps All Purpose [Plain] Flour
Pinch salt
3 Tbsps cold butter
3 Tbsps Vegetable Shortening [Stork Margarine]

2 -5 Tbsps Cold Milk
1 egg white

For custard:

3 medium eggs
1 egg yolk
1 cup milk (full fat, whole)

4 slices bacon, cooked
3-4 spring onions [green onions] or 1/4 cup chopped onions
3/4 cup grated mature cheddar cheese
1/4 teaspoon garlic granules or powder (not garlic salt!)
1/4 teaspoon ground nutmeg

Prepare quiche crust as directed in recipe (page 23) including spreading the egg white over pastry.

Cut bacon into pieces and spread evenly around quiche dish bottom. Chop onions and spread a second layer. Sprinkle grated cheese evenly.

Start the oven at gas mark 7 [450 F, 220 C].
Mix custard as directed in recipe (page 24), mixing with garlic and nutmeg.

Pour custard mixture evenly over filling. Carefully place the quiche dish in pre-heated, hot oven.

After 10 minutes, reduce heat to gas mark 4 [300 F, 150 C] and allow to bake 30-40 minutes, until golden brown on top and a knife inserted into the middle comes out clean.

Remove from oven and allow to cool 10 minutes before serving.

Spinach and Ricotta Quiche

Ingredients:

For crust:

1 cup + 2 Tbsps All Purpose [Plain] Flour
Pinch salt
3 Tbsps cold butter
3 Tbsps Vegetable Shortening [Stork Margarine]
2 -5 Tbsps Cold Milk
1 egg white

For custard:

3 medium eggs
1 egg yolk
1 cup milk (full fat, whole)
Seasonings to taste*

1 package fresh spinach leaves
1 carton Ricotta cheese - Alt: 3/4 cup grated mature cheddar cheese
1/4 teaspoon garlic granules or powder (not garlic salt!)
1/4 teaspoon ground nutmeg

Prepare quiche crust as directed in recipe (page 23) including spreading the egg white over pastry.

Wash spinach leaves in cold water. Shake out as much moisture as possible and cook in saucepan, stirring constantly. More water will appear. Allow to cool a bit, then squeeze out as much water as possible. Arrange evenly in prepared quiche crust.

Whip Ricotta cheese lightly with a spoon and drop dollops evenly over spinach.

Start the oven at gas mark 7 [450 F, 220 C].
Mix custard as directed in recipe (page 24).

Pour custard mixture evenly over filling. Carefully place the quiche dish in pre-heated, hot oven.

After 10 minutes, reduce heat to gas mark 4 [300 F, 150 C] and allow to bake 30-40 minutes, until golden brown on top and a knife inserted into the middle comes out clean.

Remove from oven and allow to cool 10 minutes before serving.

Alternatively, you may wish to make a cheddar version. Make spinach quiche as above, leaving out the Ricotta. Once quiche is baked and knife comes out clean, spread grated cheddar cheese across the top and return to oven for approximately 5 minutes, until cheese is melted. Allow to cool 10 minutes before cutting.

German Bratwurst Quiche

Ingredients:

For crust:

1 cup + 2 Tbsps All Purpose [Plain] Flour
Pinch salt
3 Tbsps cold butter
3 Tbsps Vegetable Shortening [Stork Margarine]
2 -5 Tbsps Cold Milk
1 egg white

1/2 lb white Bratwurst
Milk to fill frying pan 1/4 inch
1/2 cup mild cheddar cheese
6-8 spring onions (green onions)

For custard:

3 medium eggs
1 egg yolk
1 cup milk (full fat, whole)
1/4 teaspoon garlic granules or powder (not garlic salt!)
1/4 teaspoon ground nutmeg
1/4 teaspoon sweet paprika

Fry Bratwurst in milk. Transfer to a plate with paper towels to drain. Do **NOT** cook until crispy, but be sure it's cooked through.

Prepare quiche crust as directed in recipe (page 23) including spreading the egg white over pastry.

Cut Bratwurst into thin slices and spread over prepared crust pastry. Cut cheese into small cubes and sprinkle over Bratwurst. Slice spring onions into finely cut pieces and spread over cheese.

Start the oven at gas mark 7 [450 F, 220 C].

Mix custard as directed in recipe including garlic, nutmeg and paprika in the mix (page 24).

Pour custard mixture evenly over filling. Carefully place the quiche dish in pre-heated, hot oven.

After 10 minutes, reduce heat to gas mark 4 [300 F, 150 C] and allow to bake 30-40 minutes, until golden brown on top and a knife inserted into the middle comes out clean.

Remove from oven and allow to cool 10 minutes before serving.

The recipe can be made with more onion if desired or with other variations, like cooked cabbage or well-drained sauerkraut.

Both can also be added as a side dish.

This goes well with a good, German beer.

Chicken Kebab Quiche

Ingredients:

For crust:

1 cup + 2 Tbsps All Purpose [Plain] Flour
Pinch salt
3 Tbsps cold butter
3 Tbsps Vegetable Shortening [Stork Margarine]
2 -5 Tbsps Cold Milk
1 egg white

2 medium chicken breasts
1/4 teaspoon salt
1/4 teaspoon garlic granules
1/2 teaspoon paprika
1/2 teaspoon mild chili powder

For custard:

3 medium eggs
1 egg yolk
1 cup milk (full fat, whole)
1/8 - 1/4 teaspoon garlic granules
Pinch of nutmeg

1/2 teaspoon cumin
1 Tablespoon parsley flakes
2 Tablespoons extra virgin olive oil
2 Tablespoons lemon juice
1/4 chopped onion (optional)

Cut chicken breasts into pieces (about 1/2 inch). Make marinade of remaining ingredients and add chicken pieces. Marinade at least 2 hours (can be done a day ahead).

Stir fry chicken in marinade. Drain oil on paper towels.

Prepare quiche crust as directed in recipe (page 23) including spreading the egg white over pastry.

Spread chicken and onion evenly over crust.

Start the oven at gas mark 7 [450 F, 220 C].
Mix custard as directed in recipe (page 24).

Pour custard mixture evenly over filling. Carefully place the quiche dish in pre-heated, hot oven.

After 10 minutes, reduce heat to gas mark 4 [300 F, 150 C] and allow to bake 30-40 minutes, until golden brown on top and a knife inserted into the middle comes out clean.

Remove from oven and allow to cool 10 minutes before serving.

*If you're feeling Mediterranean, substitute lamb for chicken but be sure to fry out all fat (or bake). Choosing lean cuts is recommended. Add fresh spinach leaves with onion.

Other optional ingredients may include:

Olives (black or green)
Feta cheese
Goat cheese

Shredded red onion (instead of white onion)
Vine tomatoes cut into small wedges
1/2 teaspoon oregano mixed into the custard

Salami and Gorgonzola Quiche

Ingredients:

For crust:	For custard:
1 cup + 2 Tbsps All Purpose [Plain] Flour	3 medium eggs
Pinch salt	1 egg yolk
3 Tbsps cold butter	1 cup milk (full fat, whole)
3 Tbsps Vegetable Shortening [Stork Margarine]	1/4 teaspoon garlic granules
2 -5 Tbsps Cold Milk	pinch of ground nutmeg
1 egg white	

10-12 thin slices German salami
3 1/2 oz. [100g] Gorgonzola cheese
Optional: 1/4 onion, slivered

Lightly fry salami to cook out the fat and transfer to a plate with paper towels to drain. Do <u>NOT</u> cook until crispy.

Prepare quiche crust as directed in recipe (page 23) including spreading the egg white over pastry.

Cut salami into 1/2 inch pieces and spread over prepared crust pastry. Cube or crumble Gorgonzola cheese over salami. If adding onion, sprinkle finely cut pieces over cheese.

Start the oven at gas mark 7 [450 F, 220 C].

Mix custard as directed in recipe including garlic and nutmeg in the mix (page 24).

Pour custard mixture evenly over filling. Carefully place the quiche dish in pre-heated, hot oven.

After 10 minutes, reduce heat to gas mark 4 [300 F, 150 C] and allow to bake 30-40 minutes, until golden brown on top and a knife inserted into the middle comes out clean.

Remove from oven and allow to cool 10 minutes before serving.

For variation, you might wish to include 1/2 tin of stewed Italian tomatoes in the filling or experiment with Italian cheeses, perhaps Mozzarella and Parmesan as topping.

For a more flavourful version, also add 1 Tablespoon Italian herb mixture to custard. You can buy pre-mixed Italian herbs or mix equal amounts: basil, thyme, rosemary, marjoram, parsley, and oregano.

Masala Quiche

Ingredients:

For crust:

1 cup + 2 Tbsps All Purpose [Plain] Flour
Pinch salt
3 Tbsps cold butter
3 Tbsps Vegetable Shortening [Stork Margarine]
2 -5 Tbsps Cold Milk
1 egg white

2 medium chicken breasts
1 tin chopped tomatoes, drained
1/4 cup ground almonds
1/2 white or yellow onion

For custard:

3 medium eggs
1 egg yolk
1 cup milk (full fat, whole)
1/2 teaspoon ground cardamom
1/2 teaspoon ground cinnamon
1/2 teaspoon garam masala
1/4 teaspoon ground black pepper
pinch of ground cloves

Prepare quiche crust as directed in recipe (page 23) including spreading the egg white over pastry.

Spread almonds over crust, then sauté onion. The secret to the rich taste is cooking the onions slowly until they are very dark. Stir drained tomatoes into onion and spread evenly over almonds.

Start the oven at gas mark 7 [450 F, 220 C].

Mix custard as directed in recipe (page 24), mixing in spices. Note while whole spices are used for Indian curries, ground spices are better suited to quiche.

Pour custard mixture evenly over filling. Carefully place the quiche dish in pre-heated, hot oven.

After 10 minutes, reduce heat to gas mark 4 [300 F, 150 C] and allow to bake 30-40 minutes, until golden brown on top and a knife inserted into the middle comes out clean.

Remove from oven and allow to cool 10 minutes before serving.

This is a particularly fragrant dish that can be served with Pilau Rice, or Naan bread. It can also be accompanied by other Indian nibbles like Onion Bajis or Samosas.

A side salad with a yogurt dressing is very compatible with this one.

Quiche Rancheros

Ingredients:

For crust:

1 cup + 2 Tbsps All Purpose [Plain] Flour
Pinch salt
3 Tbsps cold butter
3 Tbsps Vegetable Shortening [Stork Margarine]
2 -5 Tbsps Cold Milk
1 egg white

1 lb minced beef
1 envelope taco seasoning mix
1 cup Cheddar cheese, grated
1 tin chopped tomatoes, drained

For custard:

3 medium eggs
1 egg yolk
1 cup milk (full fat, whole)
1/2 teaspoon cumin
1/2 teaspoon chili powder
Optional:
1/8 teaspoon cayenne pepper

Cook beef with taco seasoning mix as directed. Put half aside to cool and save for another meal. Alternatively you can cook 1/2 pound meat and use half the envelope of seasoning mix.

Prepare quiche crust as directed in recipe (page 23) including spreading the egg white over pastry.

Spread beef, cheese and tomatoes over bottom of crust.

Start the oven at gas mark 7 [450 F, 220 C].

Mix custard as directed in recipe (page 24), whisking in spices.

Pour custard mixture evenly over filling. Carefully place the quiche dish in pre-heated, hot oven.

After 10 minutes, reduce heat to gas mark 4 [300 F, 150 C] and allow to bake 30-40 minutes, until golden brown on top and a knife inserted into the middle comes out clean.

Remove from oven and allow to cool 10 minutes before serving.

A vegetarian version of this one can be made by simply leaving out the beef and taco seasoning mix.

If you wish, you can add black beans or pinto beans for extra protein and fullness.

Be sure they are thoroughly drained of water from pre-cooking!

Beans take extra effort if you're making them from dried beans. They might need soaking overnight and extensive cooking time, unless of course you use beans from a tin. Then they just need draining and drying a few minutes on paper towels.

Spicy Spanish Quiche

Ingredients:

For crust:

1 cup + 2 Tbsps All Purpose [Plain] Flour
Pinch salt
3 Tbsps cold butter
3 Tbsps Vegetable Shortening [Stork Margarine]
2 -5 Tbsps Cold Milk
1 egg white

For custard:

3 medium eggs
1 egg yolk
1 cup milk (full fat, whole)
1 teaspoon parsley flakes
1/2 teaspoon oregano
1/2 teaspoon garlic granules
1/2 teaspoon sweet paprika
1/4 teaspoon saffron
1/8 teaspoon cayenne

1/2 lb Chorizo thinly sliced
1 Tablespoon extra virgin olive oil
2 red onions, halved and sliced
2 Tablespoons brown sugar

Optional: handful of fresh spinach leaves

Lightly fry Chorizo to cook out the fat and transfer to a plate with paper towels to drain. Do **NOT** cook until crispy.

Heat oil in a large frying pan over medium heat. Cook onion for 10 mins until very soft. Add brown sugar and cook, stirring, for 5 mins until caramelised. Leave to cool.

Prepare quiche crust as directed in recipe (page 23) including spreading the egg white over pastry.

Cut Chorizo into 1/2 inch pieces and spread over prepared crust pastry. Add sautéed onions, spreading evenly.

Start the oven at gas mark 7 [450 F, 220 C].

Mix custard as directed in recipe including parsley flakes, oregano, garlic, paprika, saffron and cayenne in the mix (page 24).

Pour custard mixture evenly over filling. Carefully place the quiche dish in pre-heated, hot oven.

After 10 minutes, reduce heat to gas mark 4 [300 F, 150 C] and allow to bake 30-40 minutes, until golden brown on top and a knife inserted into the middle comes out clean.

Remove from oven and allow to cool 10 minutes before serving.

Courgette (Zucchini) and Cheese Quiche

Ingredients:

For crust:

1 cup + 2 Tbsps All Purpose [Plain] Flour
Pinch salt
3 Tbsps cold butter
3 Tbsps Vegetable Shortening [Stork Margarine]
2 -5 Tbsps Cold Milk
1 egg white

For custard:

3 medium eggs
1 egg yolk
1 cup milk (full fat, whole)
1/4 teaspoon garlic granules
pinch of ground nutmeg

1 tablespoon extra-virgin olive oil
1/4 cup red onion
1 large garlic clove
2 medium courgettes
salt (to taste)
black pepper (to taste)

1/2 cup part-skim ricotta cheese
1/2 cup part-skim shredded mozzarella cheese
1/4 cup freshly grated Parmesan cheese
2 tablespoons chopped basil

Peel courgettes with a knife as you would a potato or carrot, then cut into 1/8-inch thin slices. Put aside.

Prepare quiche crust as directed in recipe (page 23) including spreading the egg white over pastry.

Pour olive oil into sauté pan. Cut or mince garlic and add to oil. Dice red onion and sauté with garlic for 30 seconds. Add salt and pepper to taste.

Add courgette slices and cook until just soft. Using a slotted spoon, transfer 3/4 courgette mixture into crust. Add Ricotta and Mozzarella, spreading evenly.

Start the oven at gas mark 7 [450 F, 220 C].

Mix custard as directed in recipe (page 24), whisking in basil. Pour over filling.

Top with remaining courgette and parmesan cheese.

After 10 minutes, reduce heat to gas mark 4 [300 F, 150 C] and allow to bake 30-40 minutes, until golden brown on top and a knife inserted into the middle comes out clean.

Remove from oven and allow to cool 10 minutes before serving.

Club Quiche

If you've ever had a club sandwich in an American restaurant, this collection of ingredients will be familiar. Traditionally it is made with turkey and ham, though you could substitute chicken or turkey ham for the meats. It is also normally made with processed cheese, but for this recipe I suggest a decent Cheddar.

Ingredients:

For crust:

1 cup + 2 Tbsps All Purpose [Plain] Flour
Pinch salt
3 Tbsps cold butter
3 Tbsps Vegetable Shortening [Stork Margarine]
2 -5 Tbsps Cold Milk
1 egg white

For custard:

3 medium eggs
1 egg yolk
1 cup milk (full fat, whole)
1 Tablespoon mayonnaise
1/4 teaspoon garlic granules
pinch of ground nutmeg

3 - 4 thin slices ham
3 - 4 slices cheddar cheese
3 oz. leftover roast turkey or chicken
1 fresh tomato, cut into chunks or sliced

Prepare quiche crust as directed in recipe (page 23) including spreading the egg white over pastry.

Cut ham and cheese into pieces and spread each evenly around quiche dish bottom. Shred turkey and distribute over ham and cheese. Finish with tomato layer.

Start the oven at gas mark 7 [450 F, 220 C].

Mix custard as directed in recipe (page 24), mixing with mayonnaise, garlic and nutmeg.

Pour custard mixture evenly over filling. Carefully place the quiche dish in pre-heated, hot oven.

After 10 minutes, reduce heat to gas mark 4 [300 F, 150 C] and allow to bake 30-40 minutes, until golden brown on top and a knife inserted into the middle comes out clean.

Remove from oven and allow to cool 10 minutes before serving.

You may wish to include onions, finely chopped and/or raw mushrooms in the filling. This quiche in particular goes well with a side salad.

Cheese And Tomato Quiche

This is a good, versatile dish for the vegetarians. The recipe is very basic, but other vegetables can be added if desired. What variety of cheese you choose to use can completely personalise the taste. I have a preference for Gouda myself, though Cheddar is the classic for this kind of quiche. More suggestions are given at the end.

Ingredients:

For crust:

1 cup + 2 Tbsps All Purpose [Plain] Flour
Pinch salt
3 Tbsps cold butter
3 Tbsps Vegetable Shortening [Stork Margarine]
2 -5 Tbsps Cold Milk
1 egg white

For custard:

3 medium eggs
1 egg yolk
1 cup milk (full fat, whole)
1/4 teaspoon garlic granules
pinch of ground nutmeg

4-5 oz. cheese*
2 fresh salad tomatoes, sliced
1/4 finely chopped onion or 3-4 Spring onions [green onions]
Optional: Mushrooms to taste

Prepare quiche crust as directed in recipe (page 23) including spreading the egg white over pastry.

Cut cheese into pieces or grate, then spread evenly around quiche dish bottom. Chop onions and spread a second layer. Slice tomatoes and let drain.

Start the oven at gas mark 7 [450 F, 220 C].

Mix custard as directed in recipe (page 24), mixing with garlic and nutmeg.

Pour custard mixture evenly over filling. Arrange tomato slices over the top.

Carefully place the quiche dish in pre-heated, hot oven.

After 10 minutes, reduce heat to gas mark 4 [300 F, 150 C] and allow to bake 30-40 minutes, until golden brown on top and a knife inserted into the middle comes out clean.

Remove from oven and allow to cool 10 minutes before serving.

* Cheddar or Gouda is suggested.

Variations might include Double Gloucester, Red Leicester or any other hard cheese.

For a more adventurous effect, Stilton or Gorgonzola will give this quiche a zesty flavour.

Soft cheese are also possible; Ricotta, Goat cheese, or Brie all have their own results.

If using Mozzarella or other stringy cheese, I suggest mixing with similar regional cheeses or using small amounts.

Chicken and Avocado Quiche

Ingredients:

For crust:

1 cup + 2 Tbsps All Purpose [Plain] Flour
Pinch salt
3 Tbsps cold butter
3 Tbsps Vegetable Shortening [Stork Margarine]
2 -5 Tbsps Cold Milk
1 egg white

For custard:

3 medium eggs
1 egg yolk
1 cup milk (full fat, whole)
1/4 teaspoon garlic granules
pinch of ground nutmeg

3 oz. leftover roast chicken
1 ripe avocado
1/4 finely chopped onion or 3-4 Spring onions [green onions]
Optional: 3 - 4 slices cooked bacon

Prepare quiche crust as directed in recipe (page 23) including spreading the egg white over pastry.

Shred chicken and arrange evenly around quiche dish bottom. Cut bacon (if using) into pieces and spread over chicken. Chop onions and sprinkle over layers. Cut avocado into chunks and add final layer.

Start the oven at gas mark 7 [450 F, 220 C].

Mix custard as directed in recipe (page 24), mixing with garlic and nutmeg.

Pour custard mixture evenly over filling. Carefully place the quiche dish in pre-heated, hot oven.

After 10 minutes, reduce heat to gas mark 4 [300 F, 150 C] and allow to bake 30-40 minutes, until golden brown on top and a knife inserted into the middle comes out clean.

Remove from oven and allow to cool 10 minutes before serving.

This can also be made in a vegetarian version. Instead of chicken, add cut tomatoes and/or mushrooms according to your taste.

Four Cheese Quiche

Ingredients:

For crust:

1 cup + 2 Tbsps All Purpose [Plain] Flour
Pinch salt
3 Tbsps cold butter
3 Tbsps Vegetable Shortening [Stork Margarine]
2 -5 Tbsps Cold Milk
1 egg white

Approximately 3 oz. each:
Mozzarella
Gorgonzola
Parmesan
Goat cheese or Ricotta

Optional:
3 - 4 Spring onions [green onions]

For custard:

3 medium eggs
1 egg yolk
1 cup milk (full fat, whole)
1/4 teaspoon garlic granules
pinch of ground nutmeg

This recipe presents an opportunity to use up some of those holiday cheeses that would otherwise sit in the back of the fridge and turn to mould, but be sure whatever cheeses you use are compatible.

The standard recipe four cheeses are listed here. Substitute if you feel so inclined.

Prepare quiche crust as directed in recipe (page 23) including spreading the egg white over pastry.

Cut cheeses into pieces and spread evenly around quiche dish bottom. Chop onions and spread a second layer.

Start the oven at gas mark 7 [450 F, 220 C].

Mix custard as directed in recipe (page 24), mixing with garlic and nutmeg.

Pour custard mixture evenly over filling. Carefully place the quiche dish in pre-heated, hot oven.

After 10 minutes, reduce heat to gas mark 4 [300 F, 150 C] and allow to bake 30-40 minutes, until golden brown on top and a knife inserted into the middle comes out clean.

Remove from oven and allow to cool 10 minutes before serving.

Note: If you choose to use a cheese with fragrant herbs, adjust seasonings accordingly.

Cheddar Mushroom Quiche

This is another one for the vegetarians. Mushrooms make a good protein substitute, as does cheese. If you're not a fan of many vegetables, this is a simple dish with very specific flavours.

Ingredients:

For crust:

1 cup + 2 Tbsps All Purpose [Plain] Flour
Pinch salt
3 Tbsps cold butter
3 Tbsps Vegetable Shortening [Stork Margarine]
2 -5 Tbsps Cold Milk
1 egg white

4 oz. Mature Cheddar cheese
1 oz. Mushrooms, cut into chunks

For custard:

3 medium eggs
1 egg yolk
1 cup milk (full fat, whole)
1/4 teaspoon garlic granules
pinch of ground nutmeg

Prepare quiche crust as directed in recipe (page 23) including spreading the egg white over pastry.

Cut cheese into pieces and spread evenly around quiche dish bottom. Chop mushrooms and lightly sauté in butter, then spread over cheese layer.

Start the oven at gas mark 7 [450 F, 220 C].

Mix custard as directed in recipe (page 24), mixing with garlic and nutmeg.

Pour custard mixture evenly over filling. Carefully place the quiche dish in pre-heated, hot oven.

After 10 minutes, reduce heat to gas mark 4 [300 F, 150 C] and allow to bake 30-40 minutes, until golden brown on top and a knife inserted into the middle comes out clean.

Remove from oven and allow to cool 10 minutes before serving.

Note: What sort of mushrooms you choose will affect the end flavour. This is a matter of personal taste. Common Button Mushrooms are probably the popular favourite, though Portobello Mushrooms (pictured) are similar in flavour.

Shiitake or Chestnut Mushrooms will result in a stronger mushroom-y taste.

Roasted Vegetables Quiche

This one can be made with different combinations of vegetables. A couple of combinations are suggested but feel free to add or subtract your own favourite vegetables. Using Paprika instead of nutmeg in this one livens up the overall flavour.

Ingredients:

For crust:

1 cup + 2 Tbsps All Purpose [Plain] Flour
Pinch salt
3 Tbsps cold butter
3 Tbsps Vegetable Shortening [Stork Margarine]
2 -5 Tbsps Cold Milk
1 egg white

For custard:

3 medium eggs
1 egg yolk
1 cup milk (full fat, whole)
1/4 teaspoon garlic granules
Salt and black pepper to taste
pinch of paprika

Combination A:
1.1 pounds (500 grams) butternut squash, peeled and cubed
1 medium red onion, quartered
1 medium red bell pepper, seeded and thickly sliced
1 bunch asparagus, trimmed and cut into 2-inch pieces
10 medium cherry tomatoes, halved
1/4 cup olive oil

Combination B:
1 small Red Onion, sliced
1 Bell Pepper, deseeded and sliced
1 small Courgette [Zucchini], sliced
1 tbsp Olive Oil

Prepare quiche crust as directed in recipe (page 23) including spreading the egg white over pastry.

Cut vegetables into pieces and cook in olive oil. Drain oil on paper towels. Spread vegetables evenly around quiche dish bottom.

Start the oven at gas mark 7 [450 F, 220 C].

Mix custard as directed in recipe (page 24), mixing with garlic and paprika.

Pour custard mixture evenly over filling. Carefully place the quiche dish in pre-heated, hot oven.

After 10 minutes, reduce heat to gas mark 4 [300 F, 150 C] and allow to bake 30-40 minutes, until golden brown on top and a knife inserted into the middle comes out clean.

Remove from oven and allow to cool 10 minutes before serving.

Caprese Quiche

Ingredients:

For crust:

1 cup + 2 Tbsps All Purpose [Plain] Flour
Pinch salt
3 Tbsps cold butter
3 Tbsps Vegetable Shortening [Stork Margarine]
2 -5 Tbsps Cold Milk
1 egg white

For custard:

3 medium eggs
1 egg yolk
1 cup milk (full fat, whole)
1/4 teaspoon garlic granules
pinch of ground nutmeg

2 teaspoons olive oil
1/2 yellow onion
8 ounces shredded mozzarella cheese
4 ounces shredded Parmesan cheese
1/2 pint cherry or grape tomatoes, sliced in half
1/4 cup loosely packed chopped or julienned fresh basil and additional fresh basil for topping, if desired.

Prepare quiche crust as directed in recipe (page 23) including spreading the egg white over pastry.

Cut Mozzarella into pieces and spread evenly around quiche dish bottom. Cover with Parmesan. Chop onion and spread a second layer. Add tomatoes, placing evenly. Sprinkle Basil over mixture.

Start the oven at gas mark 7 [450 F, 220 C].

Mix custard as directed in recipe (page 24), mixing with garlic and nutmeg.

Pour custard mixture evenly over filling. Carefully place the quiche dish in pre-heated, hot oven.

After 10 minutes, reduce heat to gas mark 4 [300 F, 150 C] and allow to bake 30-40 minutes, until golden brown on top and a knife inserted into the middle comes out clean.

Remove from oven and allow to cool 10 minutes before serving.

Greek Olive and Goat Cheese Quiche

This recipe can work with green olives, black olives or a combination of both. I recommend buying pitted olives or olive slices. Feta cheese has a specific sharp flavour and is made from sheep or goat milk. I generally buy generic goat cheese for a milder effect.

How you choose to balance the different types of olives is a personal decision. you can use one or the other, or lean a mixture either way. I personally lean towards green for this and get the kind with Pimento for that little extra push of flavour. Be sure to drain them before adding to quiche.

In a pinch you could substitute cherry tomatoes for the Italian kind, but it's worth getting the Italian ones if possible in my opinion.

Ingredients:

For crust:

1 cup + 2 Tbsps All Purpose [Plain] Flour
Pinch salt
3 Tbsps cold butter
3 Tbsps Vegetable Shortening [Stork Margarine]
2 -5 Tbsps Cold Milk
1 egg white

For custard:

3 medium eggs
1 egg yolk
1 cup milk (full fat, whole)
1/4 teaspoon garlic granules
pinch of ground nutmeg

4 oz. Olives (green, black or both)
1 cup fresh Italian tomatoes
3 oz. Goat or Feta cheese

Prepare quiche crust as directed in recipe (page 23) including spreading the egg white over pastry.

Cut cheese into pieces and spread evenly around quiche dish bottom. Cut olives in half and Make sure they are without pits. Spread a second layer. Cut tomatoes into pieces and arrange evenly.

Start the oven at gas mark 7 [450 F, 220 C].

Mix custard as directed in recipe (page 24), mixing with garlic and nutmeg.

Pour custard mixture evenly over filling. Carefully place the quiche dish in pre-heated, hot oven.

After 10 minutes, reduce heat to gas mark 4 [300 F, 150 C] and allow to bake 30-40 minutes, until golden brown on top and a knife inserted into the middle comes out clean.

Remove from oven and allow to cool 10 minutes before serving.

Cajun Quiche

This recipe is subject to many variations. I've given a sausage quiche, but you may wish to make it with cooked prawns, crawfish or spiced chicken. Andouille sausage is particular to Louisiana, so may be difficult to find elsewhere.

One important element of Cajun cooking is layering spices. If you are frying chicken pieces or seafood, add spice each time you turn the meat. This isn't necessary with the spiced sausage option as the spices are already included in the sausage making process.

Louisiana cooking is different than anywhere else because of methods like this, developed over centuries of a unique combination of multi-cultural cooking.

Ingredients:

For crust:

1 cup + 2 Tbsps All Purpose [Plain] Flour
Pinch salt
3 Tbsps cold butter
3 Tbsps Vegetable Shortening [Stork Margarine]
2 -5 Tbsps Cold Milk
1 egg white

For custard:

3 medium eggs
1 egg yolk
1 cup milk (full fat, whole)
1 teaspoon Cajun seasoning

200 grams Andouille sausage	Cajun spice:
* or substitute Kielbasa sausage	
1 tin chopped tomatoes, drained	2 teaspoons salt
4-6 spring [green] onions, chopped	2 teaspoons garlic powder
1-2 teaspoons mixed Cajun spice	2 1/2 teaspoons paprika
	1 teaspoon ground black pepper
You can use Cajun spice mix from	1 teaspoon onion powder
the supermarket, or mix your own:	1 teaspoon cayenne pepper
	1 1/4 teaspoons dried oregano
	1 1/4 teaspoons dried thyme

Prepare quiche crust as directed in recipe (page 23) including spreading the egg white over pastry.

Slice sausage thinly and spread around crust bottom. Add tomatoes and sprinkle chopped onion.

Start the oven at gas mark 7 [450 F, 220 C].

Mix custard as directed in recipe (page 24), mixing in Cajun spice.

Pour custard mixture evenly over filling. Carefully place the quiche dish in pre-heated, hot oven.

After 10 minutes, reduce heat to gas mark 4 [300 F, 150 C] and allow to bake 30-40 minutes, until golden brown on top and a knife inserted into the middle comes out clean.

Remove from oven and allow to cool 10 minutes before serving.

NOTE: To get a really authentic taste of Louisiana, you might want to add finely chopped bell pepper and celery to the filling. Those and onion are known as the holy trinity of Louisiana cooking, as they form the basis for many of the popular dishes from the area.

Savoury Pumpkin Quiche

This quiche is similar to Pumpkin Pie, but not as sweet and is suitable as a main dish.

Ingredients:

For crust:

1 cup + 2 Tbsps All Purpose [Plain] Flour
Pinch salt
3 Tbsps cold butter
3 Tbsps Vegetable Shortening [Stork Margarine]
2 -5 Tbsps Cold Milk
1 egg white

For custard:

One tin pureed pumpkin
One tin evaporated milk
2 eggs
pinch of salt
2 teaspoons Pumpkin pie spice

Prepare quiche crust as directed in recipe (page 23) excluding spreading egg white over the pastry.

Start the oven at gas mark 7 [450 F, 220 C].

This one is a little different in that evaporated milk is used and the filling and custard stage is all one. Whisk eggs in a large bowl, then add pumpkin, salt and spice. Whisk in evaporated milk and pour into prepared quiche pastry.

You may have some filling left over. I usually use a ramekin to bake this and with a couple of spoons of sugar, it makes a lovely pumpkin pudding! Do not over fill the quiche crust.

Carefully place the quiche dish in pre-heated, hot oven.

After 15 minutes, reduce heat to gas mark 5 [350 F, 175 C] and allow to bake 30-40 minutes, until brown on top and a knife inserted into the middle comes out clean.

Remove from oven and allow to cool 10 minutes before serving.

* Note: You can make this with fresh pumpkin, but I find it rather a large amount of work and fuss. Save your sanity and buy the tinned pumpkin!

Pumpkin Pie Spice

4 tablespoons cinnamon
1 teaspoon ground ginger
1/2 teaspoon ground nutmeg
1/4 teaspoon ground cloves
1/4 teaspoon ground all-spice

Combine the cinnamon, nutmeg, cloves, all-spice and ginger together.
Store in an airtight container for up to 12 months.

You can use store bought pumpkin pie spice if you live in the US, but use one teaspoon of pumpkin pie spice and one teaspoon of cinnamon. This gives you the right flavour combination for an optimum pumpkin pie or quiche.

Pumpkin Pie

Now that you have Pumpkin Pie Spice, it would be remiss of me to leave out my Pumpkin Pie recipe, although it isn't a quiche. The concept is very similar and besides, a friend asked me to include it.

The important thing to remember is that crust for quiche is very different from a crust you would use for a dessert pie. You may already have a favourite crust recipe for oil pastry or using shortening. Feel free to use this, but whatever you do, do NOT buy a pre-made crust. They're awful, tasteless, have a texture like cardboard and would spoil the whole pie experience.

I use a basic English shortcrust recipe as follows:

>Ingredients:
>
>8 oz. plain (all purpose) flour
>pinch salt
>1 oz. sugar
>2 oz. lard
>2 oz margarine
>Ice cold water to mix (approximately 2 Tablespoons)

Mix flour, sugar and salt in a medium but wide bowl. Cut in fats with a pastry cutter and rub with fingers until the texture of fine meal. Stir in cold water with a fork until the dough holds together. Knead lightly in bowl.

Like the quiche crust, I prefer to press it into the pie plate rather than roll it out and try to keep it together to transfer. Be sure to press it thin.

Filling Ingredients:

3/4 cup white sugar
1 teaspoon ground cinnamon
1 teaspoon Pumpkin Pie Spice (page)
1/2 teaspoon salt
2 large eggs
1 (15 ounce) can Pumpkin
1 (12 fluid ounce) can Evaporated Milk

Start the oven at gas mark 7 [450 F, 220 C].

Whisk eggs in a large bowl. Stir in sugar and spices, still using the hand whisk. Add pumpkin, stirring thoroughly. Add evaporated milk a little at a time until all is mixed in. Pour into pie shell and bake for 15 minutes, then reduce heat to gas mark 5 [350 F, 175 C] and allow to bake 30-40 minutes, until brown on top and a knife inserted into the middle comes out clean.

Allow to cool before cutting.

Custom Quiche

By now you've got the idea of how to make a magnificent quiche and that you can customise it to your personal taste. Now it's time to make your own signature quiche!

Ingredients:

For crust:

1 cup + 2 Tbsps All Purpose [Plain] Flour
Pinch salt
3 Tbsps cold butter
3 Tbsps Vegetable Shortening [Stork Margarine]
2 -5 Tbsps Cold Milk
1 egg white

For custard:

3 medium eggs
1 egg yolk
1 cup milk (full fat, whole)
Seasonings to taste*

Quiche crust (page 23)
Custard mix (page 24)
Meats and/or vegetables of your choice
Seasonings of your choice

Prepare quiche crust as directed in recipe (page 23) including spreading the egg white over pastry.

Arrange filling ingredients of your choice over crust bottom.

Start the oven at gas mark 7 [450 F, 220 C].

Mix custard as directed in recipe (page 24), adding in any seasonings you wish.

Pour custard mixture evenly over filling. Carefully place the quiche dish in pre-heated, hot oven.

After 10 minutes, reduce heat to gas mark 4 [300 F, 150 C] and allow to bake 30-40 minutes, until golden brown on top and a knife inserted into the middle comes out clean.

Remove from oven and allow to cool 10 minutes before serving.

Ingredients That Must Be Cooked First

All meats must be drained of excess fat

Minced beef (spiced?)	Spinach
Minced pork	Broccoli
Shredded chicken	Okra
Pepperoni, well drained	Cabbage or red cabbage
Salami, fried & well drained	Squash (all kinds)
Fish	
Ham	Most other vegetables
Sausage	
Bacon	

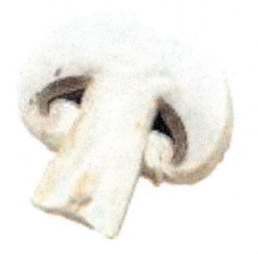

Ingredients That Can Be Cooked or Raw
Mushrooms
Bell pepper (slices, recommend parboiled)
Tomatoes

Ingredients To Add Raw

Onions	Cheese (All kinds)
Spring onions [green onions]	Pepperoncini peppers
Olives	Jalapeños

If in doubt, note most ingredients should be cooked in advance.

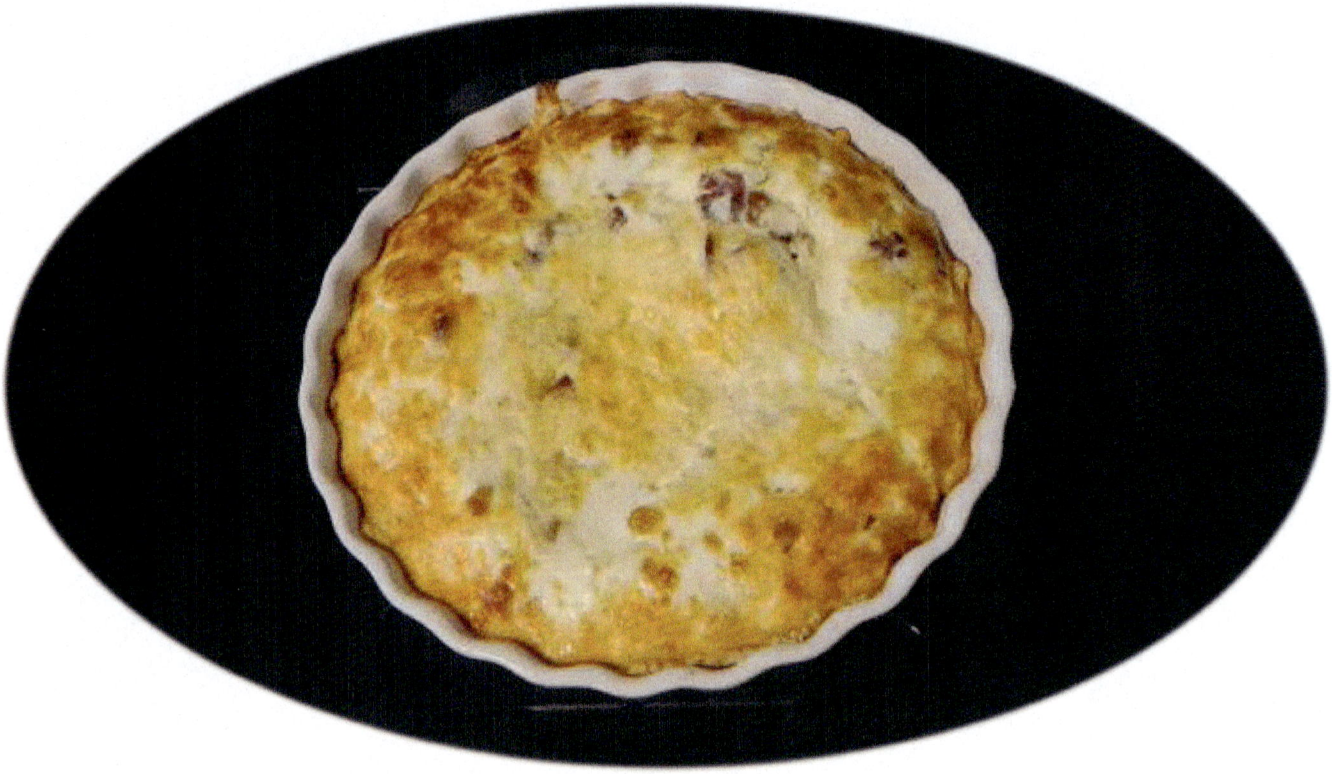

A World of Possibilities

There you have it. A world of flavour possibilities awaits for you to experiment, perhaps make a few mistakes, and discover your own special recipes to suit your own individual taste.

Please do take chances, not only with filling ingredients but also with seasoning combinations that have appealed to you in other recipes.

There are no rules for what can be included in a quiche. Just remember to avoid excess fluids or liquid grease, as these will interfere with the custard setting.

I hope you've enjoyed this book and that you'll tell your friends about it. As with any book, a quick review online will help other readers discover this amazing world of culinary delight.

My Own Unique Recipes

Printed in Great Britain
by Amazon